DARE TO EXCEL

Compiled by:
Diane Voreis

Cover Illustration by Design Dynamics

Published by Great Quotations Publishing Company
Downers Grove, IL

Library of Congress Catalog number: 99-072990
ISBN: 1-56245-384-X

Printed in Hong Kong 2001

FOREWORD

This collection of quotations provides us with the thoughts of those who dared to excel, to reach the top. Excellence is a choice available to all in whatever endeavors we choose to pursue.

Oliver Wendell Holmes said it best, "Man's mind stretched to a new idea, never goes back to its original dimensions." So too it is with achievement. Once stretched the capacity remains and even grows. Begin the extra effort now. Dare to excel.

If a man is called to be a streetsweeper, he should sweep streets even as Michelangelo painted, or Beethoven composed music, or Shakespeare wrote poetry. He should sweep streets so well that all the hosts of heaven and earth will pause to say, here lived a great streetsweeper who did his job well.

Martin Luther King, Jr.

4

The quality of a person's life is in direct proportion
to their commitment to excellence, regardless of
their chosen field of endeavor.

Vince Lombardi

Excellence means when a man or woman asks of himself more than others do.

Ortega & Gassett

6

To be what we are, and to become what we are capable of becoming, is the only end of life.

Robert Louis Stevenson

All successful employers are stalking men who will do the unusual, men who think, men who attract attention by performing more than is expected of them.

Charles M. Schwab

More powerful than all the success slogans ever penned by human hand is the realization for every man that he has but one boss. That boss is the man-- he--himself.

Gabriel Heatter

There is a kind of elevation which does not depend on fortune; it is a certain air which distinguishes us, and seems to destine us for great things; it is a price which we imperceptibly set upon ourselves.

Francois De La Rochefoucauld

Hold yourself responsible for a higher standard than anybody else expects of you. Never excuse yourself.

Henry Ward Beecher

You gain strength, courage and confidence by every experience in which you must stop and look fear in the face...You must do the thing you think you cannot do.

Eleanor Roosevelt

It sometimes seems that intense desire creates not only its own opportunities, but its own talents.

Eric Hoffer

You can have anything you want- if you want it badly enough.. You can be anything you want to be, have anything you desire, accomplish anything you set out to accomplish - if you will hold to that desire with singleness of purpose...

Robert Collier

To many a man, and sometimes to a youth, there comes the opportunity to choose between honorable competence and tainted wealth...The young man who starts out to be poor and honorable, holds in his hand one of the strongest elements of success.

Orison Swett Marden

You see things; and say "Why?" But I dreams things that never were; and I say, "Why not?"

George Bernard Shaw

Cherish your visions and your dreams as they are the children of your soul; the blue prints of your ultimate achievements.

Napoleon Hill

The only limit to our realization of tomorrow will be our doubts of today.

Franklin D. Roosevelt

Life is my college.

Louisa May Alcott

Life is a series of experiences, each one of which makes us bigger, even though sometimes it is hard to realize this. For the world was built to develop character, and we must learn that the setbacks and griefs which we endure help us in our marching onward.

Henry Ford

The more one works, the more willing one is to work.

Lord Chesterfield

The first step is the hardest.

Marie De Vichy-Chamrond

Do not wait; the time will never be "just right."
Start where you stand, and work with whatever tools
you may have at your command, and better tools
will be found as you go along.

Napoleon Hill

Give yourself something to work toward-constantly.

Mary Kay Ash

What's important is that one strives to achieve a goal.

Ronald Reagan

Daring ideas are like chessmen, moved forward: they may be beaten, but they may start a winning game.

Johann Wolfgang Von Goethe

If a man does not keep pace with his companions, perhaps it is because he hears a different drummer. Let him step to the music which he hears, however measured or far away.

Henry David Thoreau

First say to yourself what you would be; and then do what you have to do.

Epictetus

As fast as each opportunity presents itself, use it! No matter how tiny an opportunity it may be, use it!

Robert Collier

Destiny is not a matter of chance: it is a matter of choice. It is not something to be waited for: but rather something to be achieved.

William Jennings Bryan

We all have possibilities we don't know about. We can do things we don't even dream we can do.

Dale Carnegie

31

If we all did the things we are capable of doing, we would literally astound ourselves.

Thomas A. Edison

Everyone has inside of him a piece of good news,
The good news is that you don't know how great
you can be! How much you can love! What you can
accomplish! And what your potential is!

Anne Frank

Within you right now is the power to do things you never dreamed possible. This power becomes available to you just as soon as you can change your beliefs.

Maxwell Maltz

No one knows what he can do till he tries.

Publilius Syrus

There is always room at the top.

Daniel Webster

Few things in the world are more powerful than a positive push. A smile. A word of optimism and hope. A "you can do it" when things are tough.

Richard M. DeVos

Perhaps the most valuable result of all education is the ability to make yourself do the thing you have to do, when it ought to be done, whether you like it or not. It is the first lesson that ought to be learned.

Thomas H. Huxley

There is no victory at bargain basement prices.

Dwight David Eisenhower

Life will always be to a large extent what we ourselves make it.

Samuel Smiles

No person was ever honored for what he received:
honor has been the reward for what he gave.

Calvin Coolidge

I made a resolve then that I was going to amount to something if I could. And no hours, nor amount of labor, nor amount of money would deter me from giving the best that there was in me. And I have done that ever since, and I win by it. I know.

Colonel Harland Sanders

I want you to start a crusade in your life--to dare to be your best.

William Danforth

It's the repetition of...affirmations that leads to belief. And once that belief become a deep conviction, things begin to happen.

Claude M. Bristol

Set priorities for your goals...A major part of successful living lies in the ability to put first things first. Indeed, the reason most major goals are not achieved is that we spend our time doing second things first.

Robert J. McKain

Our aspirations are our possibilities.

Robert Browning

The more you can dream, the more you can do.

Michael Korda

Dream no small dreams for they have no power to move the hearts of men.

Johann Wolfgang Von Goethe

Your expectation opens or closes the doors of your supply. If you expect grand things, and work honestly for them, they will come to you, your supply will correspond with your expectation.

Orison Swett Marden

If you think you can win, you can win. Faith is necessary to victory.

William Hazlitt

Always do more than is required of you.

George S. Patton

You don't concentrate on risks. You concentrate on results. No risk is too great to prevent the necessary job from getting done.

Chuck Yeager

Chance favors the prepared mind.

Louis Pasteur

No one ever attains very eminent success by simply doing what is required of him; it is the amount and excellence of what is over and above the required, that determines the greatness of ultimate distinction.

Charles Kendall Adams

The world is a looking-glass, and gives back to every man the reflection of his own face. Frown at it, and it in turn will look sourly upon you; laugh at it and with it, and it is a jolly, kind companion.

William Makespeace Thackeray

Always ask why you're doing anything. Be kind, especially if you have a gift. Be honest. Take risks.

Yo-Yo Ma

Music is your own experience--your thoughts, your wisdom. If you don't live it, it won't come out of your horn.

Charlie Parker

Be daring, be different, be impractical; be anything that will assert integrity of purpose and imaginative vision against the play-it-safers, the creatures of the commonplace, the slaves of the ordinary. Routines have their purposes, but the merely routine is the hidden enemy of high art.

Cecil Beaton

The artist who aims at perfection in everything
achieves it in nothing.

Eugene Delacroix

Goals are dreams with deadlines.

Ken Blanchard

Always listen to experts. They'll tell you what can't be done and why. Then do it.

Robert Heinlein

The key is not the "will to win"... everybody has that.
It is the will to *prepare* to win that is important.

Bobby Knight

Always do right. This will gratify some people and astonish the rest.

Mark Twain

Enthusiasm reflects confidence, spreads good cheer, raises morale, inspires associates, arouses loyalty, and laughs at adversity...it is beyond the price.

Alan Cox

All growth is a leap in the dark, an intuitive guess backed by knowledge and experience.

Henry Miller

No one can arrive from being talented alone. God gives talent, work transforms talent into genius.

Anna Pavlova

Don't compromise yourself. You are all you've got.

Janis Joplin

I do not know anyone who has got to the top
without hard work. That is the recipe. It will not
always get you to the top, but should get you pretty
near.

Margaret Thatcher

Three outstanding qualities make for success: judgement, industry, health. And the greatest of these is judgment.

William Maxwell Aitken

Do something every day that you don't want to do;
this is the golden rule of acquiring the habit of
doing your duty without pain.

Mark Twain

No pessimist ever discovered the secrets of the stars,
or sailed to an uncharted land, or opened a new
heaven to the human spirit.

Helen Keller

To live each day as though one's last, never flustered, never apathetic, never attitudinizing - here is the perfection of character.

Marcus Aurelius

It had long since come to my attention that people of accomplishment rarely sat back and let things happen to them. They went out and happened to things.

Elinor Smith

You may be disappointed if you fail, but you are doomed if you don't try.

Beverly Sills

Think of these things; whence you came, where you are going, and to whom you must account.

Benjamin Franklin

I think it's the end of progress if you stand still and think of what you've done in the past. I keep on.

Leslie Caron

76

All serious daring starts from within.

Eudora Welty

This above all: To thine own self be true, and it must follow, as the night the day, thou canst not then be false to any man.

William Shakespeare

The secret of joy in work is contained in one word--
excellence. To know how to do something well is to
enjoy it.

Pearl Buck

The credit belongs to the man who is actually in the arena, who strives valiantly;...who knows the great enthusiasms, the great devotions,...and spends himself in a worthy cause, who at the best, knows the triumph of high achievement; and who, at the worst, if he fails,...at least fails while daring greatly, so that his place shall never be with those cold and timid souls...who know neither victory nor defeat.

Theodore Roosevelt

You can't solve a problem with the same type of thinking which created it.

Albert Einstein

There is a loftier ambition than merely to stand high in the world. It is to stoop down and lift mankind a little higher.

Henry Van Dyke

Always bear in mind that your own resolution to succeed is more important than any other one thing.

Abraham Lincoln

Personal relationships are the fertile soil from which all advancement, all success, all achievement in real life grows.

Ben Stein

You can have everything in life you want, if you will just help enough people get what they want.

Zig Ziglar

You measure the size of the accomplishment by the obstacles you had to overcome to reach your goals.

Booker T. Washington

Winners will take care of themselves. When you give your best effort, that is what makes you a winner.

John Wooden

Character may be manifested in the great moments, but it is made in the small ones.

Phillips Brooks

Surely a man has come to himself only when he has found the best that is in him, and has satisfied his heart with the highest achievement he is fit for.

Woodrow Wilson

Don't bother about genius. Don't worry about being clever. Place your trust in hard work, enthusiasm, perseverance and determination.

Sir Frederick Treves

If you think you can, you can. If you think you can't, you're right.

Mary Kay Ash

The excellent becomes the permanent.

Jane Addams

Everyone's got it in him, if he'll only make up his mind and stick at it. None of us is born with a stop-valve on his powers or with a set limit to his capacities. There's no limit possible to the expansion of each one of us.

Charles M. Schwab

In all human affairs there are efforts and there are results, and the strength of the effort is the measure of the result.

William Edward

Life is about not knowing, having to change, taking the moment and making the best of it, without knowing what's going to happen next. Delicious ambiguity.

Gilda Radner

The human spirit needs to accomplish, to achieve, to triumph to be happy.

Ben Stein

Sometimes if you want to see a change for the better, you have to take things into your own hands.

Clint Eastwood

You have a good many little gifts and virtues, but there is no need of parading them, for conceit spoils the finest genius. There is not much danger that real talent or goodness will be overlooked long, and the great charm of all power is modesty.

Louisa May Alcott

Only those who dare to fail greatly can ever achieve greatly.

Robert Kennedy

Never turn down a job because you think it's too small, you don't know where it can lead.

Julia Morgan

To me success means effectiveness in the world, that I am able to carry my ideas and values into the world- that I am able to change it in positive ways.

Maxine Hong Kingston

The secret of success is consistency of purpose.

Benjamin Disraeli

Nothing great was ever achieved without enthusiasm.

Ralph Waldo Emerson

There is something that is much more scarce,
something rarer than ability. It is the ability to
recognize ability.

Robert Half

The best executive is the one who has the sense
enough to pick good men to do what he wants done,
and self-restraint enough to keep from meddling
with them while they do it.

Theodore Roosevelt

The man who makes no mistakes does not usually make anything.

Bishop W.C. Magee

Do not let what you cannot do interfere with what you can do.

John Wooden

I'm a great believer in luck, and I find the harder I
work the more I have of it.

Thomas Jefferson

It is never too late to be what you might have become.

George Eliot

It's hard to detect good luck--it looks so much like something you've earned.

Frank A. Clark

There is no security on this earth, only opportunity.

Douglas MacArthur

The measure of success is not whether you have a tough problem to deal with, but whether it's the same problem you had last year.

John Foster Dulles

Minds are like parachutes; they only function when open.

Lord Dewar

Genius is the ability to reduce the complicated to the simple.

C.W. Ceran

One man with courage makes a majority.

Andrew Jackson

When you cannot make up your mind which of two evenly balanced courses of action you should take- choose the bolder one.

W.J. Slim

Many things are lost for want of asking.

English Proverb

The world stands aside to let anyone pass who knows where he is going.

David Jordan

The price of greatness is responsibility.

Winston Churchill

Nurture your mind with great thoughts. To believe in the heroic makes heroes.

Benjamin Disraeli

The right man is the one who seizes the moment.

Johann Wolfgang Von Goethe

The highest reward for a person's toil is not what they get for it, but what they become by it.

John Ruskin

The greatest ability is dependability.

Curt Bergwall

The art of being wise is the art of knowing what to overlook.

William James

Wisdom consists of knowing what to do next; virtue in doing it.

David Starr Jordan

Progress involves risks. You can't steal second and keep your foot on first.

Frederick Wilcox

Take calculated risks. That is quite different from being rash.

General George S. Patton, Jr.

It's not half as important to burn the midnight oil
as it is to be awake in daytime.

E.W. Elmore

You can be an ordinary athlete by getting away with less than your best. But if you want to be one of the greats, you have to give it all you've got--your everything.

Duke Kahanamoku

The superior man makes the difficulty to be
overcome his first interest; success only comes later.

Confucius

I'm a firm believer that people only do their best at things they truly enjoy. It's difficult to excel at something you don't enjoy.

Jack Nicklaus

Commitment is the willingness to do whatever it takes to get what you want. A true commitment is a heartfelt promise to yourself from which you will not back down. Many people have dreams and many have good intentions but few are willing to make the commitment for their attainment.

David McNally

Even when I went to the playground, I never picked the best players. I picked the guys with less talent, but who were willing to work hard...and put in the effort, who had the desire to be great.

Earvin "Magic" Johnson

Nothing splendid has ever been achieved except by those who dared believe that something inside of them was superior to circumstance.

Bruce Barton

Common sense is perhaps the most equally divided but surely the most under-employed talent in the world.

Christine Collange

One characteristic of successful people from all walks of life is their internal accountability--they see themselves as responsible for gaining the excellence they seek and look inside for the strengths with which to achieve it.

Sidney Lecker

136

The basic foundation of excellence lies in personal pride, energy and enthusiasm.

Dr. Dan Leimann

Vision is the art of seeing the invisible.

Jonathan Swift

Windows of opportunity exist for only a brief moment in time, you have to have vision in order to spot them, and take advantage of them.

John Sculley

If one is lucky, a solitary fantasy can totally transform one million realities.

Maya Angelou

Garden variety, everyday passion is the stuff of excellence.

Tom Peters & Nancy Austin

141

We must continually expand our realm of knowledge and our field of vision through the thorough digestion and incorporation of new information.

M. Scott Peck

The mind is everything; what you think, you become.

Buddha

Even a small star shines in the darkness.

Finnish Proverb

The most important thing in communication is to hear what isn't being said.

Peter Drucker

145

Live your life so that your autograph will be wanted instead of your fingerprints.

Howard Duckly

If at first you don't succeed, try, try again.

William Edward Hickson

It's not whether you get knocked down, it's whether
you get up.

Vincent Lombardi

To make it to the top, you've got to want it with all your heart.

Linda Wachman

Great minds discuss ideas, average minds discuss events, small minds discuss people.

Laurence J. Peter

Keep away from people who try to belittle your ambitions. Small people always do that, but the really great make you feel that you, too, can become great.

Mark Twain

There is something more important than believing: **ACTION!**

The world is full of dreamers, there aren't enough who will move ahead and begin to take concrete steps to actualize their vision.

W. Clement Stone

If a man writes a better book, preaches a better sermon, or makes a better mousetrap than his neighbor, though he builds his house in the woods, the world will make a beaten path to his door.

Ralph Waldo Emerson

153

You are the same today that you are going to be five years from now except for two things: The people with whom you associate and the books you read.

Charles "Tremendous" Jones

154

Inspiration does not come like a bolt, nor is it kinetic, energetic striving, but it comes into us slowly and quietly and all the time, though we must regularly and every day give it a little chance to start flowing.

Brenda Ueland

Enthusiasm is the electricity of life. How do you get it? Act enthusiastic and you'll become enthusiastic.

Dale Carnegie

A really great person is known by three signs: generosity in the design, humanity in the execution and moderation in success.

Otto Bismarck

Perfection consists not in doing extraordinary things, but in doing ordinary things extraordinarily well. Neglect nothing.

Angelique Arnauld

When you get right down to the root of the meaning of the word "succeed" you find that it simply means "follow through".

F. W. Nichol

If you wish your merit to be known, acknowledge that of other people.

Chinese Proverb

Adversity brings out talents that prosperity overlooks.

Horace

The spirit, the will to win, and the will to excel are things that endure. These qualities are so much more important than the events that occur.

Vince Lombardi

Push yourself again and again. Don't give an inch
until the final buzzer sounds.

Larry Bird

Ability may get you to the top, but it takes character to keep you there.

John Wooden

Well done is better than well said.
Benjamin Franklin

Whatever you do or dream you can do - begin it.
Boldness has genius and power and magic in it.

Johann Wolfgang Von Goethe

Just make up your mind at the very outset that your work is going to stand for quality...that you are going to stamp a superior quality upon everything that goes out of your hands, that whatever you do shall bear the hall-mark of excellence.

Orison Swett Marden

Other Titles by Great Quotations

301 Ways to Stay Young At Heart
African-American Wisdom
A Lifetime of Love
A Light Heart Lives Long
Angel-grams
As A Cat Thinketh
A Servant's Heart
Astrology for Cats
Astrology for Dogs
A Teacher is Better Than Two Books
A Touch of Friendship
Can We Talk
Celebrating Women
Chicken Soup
Chocoholic Reasonettes
Daddy & Me
Dare to Excel
Erasing My Sanity
Falling in Love
Fantastic Father, Dependable Dad
Golden Years, Golden Words
Graduation Is Just The Beginning
Grandma, I Love You
Happiness is Found Along The Way

High Anxieties
Hooked on Golf
I Didn't Do It
Ignorance is Bliss
I'm Not Over the Hill
Inspirations
Interior Design for Idiots
Let's Talk Decorating
Life's Lessons
Life's Simple Pleasures
Looking for Mr. Right
Midwest Wisdom
Mommy & Me
Mom's Homemade Jams
Mother, I Love You
Motivating Quotes for Motivated People
Mrs. Murphy's Laws
Mrs. Webster's Dictionary
My Daughter, My Special Friend
Only a Sister
Parenting 101
Pink Power
Read the Fine Print

Reflections
Romantic Rhapsody
Size Counts !
Social Disgraces
Sports Prose
Stress or Sanity
The ABC's of Parenting
The Be-Attitudes
The Birthday Astrologer
The Cornerstones of Success
The Rose Mystique
The Secret Language of Men
The Secret Language of Women
The Secrets in Your Face
The Secrets in Your Name
TeenAge of Insanity
Thanks from the Heart
The Lemonade Handbook
The Mother Load
The Other Species
Wedding Wonders
Words From The Coach
Working Woman's World

Great Quotations Publishing Company
2800 Centre Circle
Downers Grove, IL 60515, U.S.A.
Phone: 630-268-9900   Fax: 630-268-9500